THE MOST INSPIRATIONAL BASKETBALL STORIES
FOR YOUNG READERS

15

AMAZING & INSPIRING

TRUE TALES

FROM MODERN BASKETBALL GREATS

TERRENCE ARMSTRONG

CONTENTS

INTRODUCTION

"I've failed over and over and over again in my life.
And that is why I succeed."
— *Michael Jordan*

Success and failure go hand in hand, and the journey to victory is often marked by setbacks and disappointments. You will face self-doubt, challenges, and demotivation, but if you choose to rise again, you are bound to achieve remarkable things.

The world of basketball is full of inspiring stories. There are athletes who, despite the odds, achieved greatness. They faced injuries, battled challenges, and achieved greatness. How did they do it? What made them different? What was their defining moment? All of this is exactly what we will be talking about in this book.

These success stories show that if you remain dedicated, work hard, and believe in yourself, you can achieve anything. We hope these stories will inspire you to keep chasing your goals with all your heart.

So, we warmly welcome all of you hoopsters and future ball stars! Tighten those laces, because this book is about to take you on a ride through the incredible world of modern basketball greats!

You'll encounter basketball players who started out just like you—with a love for the game and a dream in their hearts. These legends pushed the game to its limits, all while dealing with their own troubles.

You'll be inspired by the mental strength and tenacity of these superstars.

In chapter 1, we'll meet LeBron James, who went from being a high school baller to a professional superhero. He's not just a legend on the court—he's a living, breathing example that dreams can come true if you give them all you've got.

Ever heard of a guy named Stephen Curry? Chapter 2 will tell the story of this three-point wizard. We'll witness how he changed the game and showed the world that sometimes you've got to shake things up to make your mark.

Our third chapter will introduce you to Derrick Rose, the comeback king. His story isn't just about bouncing back from tough times—it's about turning setbacks and failures into setups for success. Trust us, you're in for an amazing tale.

Chapter 4 is about Kevin Durant, the quiet giant who lets his incredible skills do the talking. His story proves that you don't need to be loud to be heard—you just need to leave your mark on the game.

In chapter 5, maestro Chris Paul takes the stage. His work ethic and technique teach the importance of teamwork, leadership, and the pursuit of excellence.

And how could we forget Dirk Nowitzki, the Maverick's legend? In chapter 6, you'll discover how he shattered stereotypes and transcended borders, proving to us that greatness has no limits.

Chapter 7 is about Kawhi Leonard. His story teaches us many valuable lessons, including the fact that true strength involves facing challenges with silent resilience.

Chapter 8 unfolds the story of Giannis Antetokounmpo, the Greek Freak. His journey is a celebration of being unique and embracing your individual strengths.

In chapter 9, we'll meet Russell Westbrook, the triple-double machine. His high-energy tale teaches us that success isn't only about winning. It's also about giving it your all, every single time.

You are in for a treat in chapter 10, which explores the lasting impact of Kobe Bryant, a basketball legend whose legacy extends well beyond the court. He's a reminder that true greatness means making a positive impact on the world.

Chapter 11 is all about the dazzling influence of Dwyane Wade, aka The Flash. His story is a fast-paced saga about determination, leadership, and lifting those around you.

Carmelo Anthony, the consistent genius, takes the spotlight in Chapter 12. His story is a symphony of skill and determination, demonstrating that success is a masterpiece crafted through consistent effort and love for the game.

Chapter 13 invites you into the world of Joel Embiid, a towering figure with inspiring resilience. His story is a canvas painted with determination, showcasing that challenges are opportunities to grow stronger.

In chapter 14, legendary Trailblazer Damian Lillard shows us the power of clutch performances. It's not just about talent—it's about rising to the occasion when the spotlight is brightest.

And in our final chapter, Kyle Lowry steps into the spotlight, transitioning from hardwood to leadership positions. His story is a classic example of how perseverance can transform a player into a leader, making a positive impact in their communities.

As we journey through these awesome stories, imagine yourself courtside, absorbing the electrifying energy with every turn of the page. Each chapter is like a secret playbook, revealing not just the moves on the court, but also the heart, passion, and tenacity that turned these players into legends.

LeBron, Stephen, Derrick, and the rest of the talented ballers you're about to meet weren't born shooting hoops—they were just dreamers with a passion for the game. Chapter after chapter, you will witness their highs, their lows, and the incredible comebacks that define true champions.

These 15 journeys will also show you how a sport can transform a life and serve as a guiding force towards opportunities, success, and self-realization.

Each page is a dribble closer to discovering that your dreams, no matter how big they are, are just a dunk away from becoming reality. This is something you'll discover with each story. Be it Kobe, Russell, Chris, Lillard, or any of the 15 players we've covered, all of them have had that one defining moment that propelled them to greatness!

I hope these stories will ignite the fire within you. Take a leap, make those shots, and let the court be the canvas for your dreams. Your journey has just begun, but who knows—maybe one day we'll be flipping through the pages of your story in a book like this.

That sure would be a cool thing, right?

So, let's keep that in mind and get started!

LEBRON JAMES FROM HIGH SCHOOL BASKETBALL TO NBA LEGEND

LeBron James is one of the most renowned names in basketball, but his journey to become an NBA legend was filled with lots of ups and downs. We'll walk a mile in his shoes and try to get a glimpse of everything the legend has experienced throughout his life.

To learn all that we can from the challenges he faced, we'll look at his early years growing up in Ohio, what school was ike for LeBron, his entry into the NBA, the challenges he faced, and more. We even have a dedicated section at the end with all the lessons that can be learned from his story. Let's meet LeBron James!

GROWING UP IN AKRON, OHIO

LeBron was born in Akron, Ohio, to Gloria Marie James, who at his birth was only 16. His life, even at a young age, was filled with countless challenges. Their family kept moving from one apartment to another, keeping them from having the stability they needed.

Can you imagine what it must have been like for a young kid not being able to settle down in one place? Think about how it would feel if you had to make friends while knowing that you'd soon lose them because you'd have to move somewhere else.

During his young years, LeBron grew up in some of the roughest neighborhoods of Akron. His mother had a hard time finding a job, and his father was a convicted criminal who wasn't part of the family and didn't support them financially. All of this took a toll on young LeBron, and this isn't something that went unnoticed by his mother.

Trying to shield her son from all that was going on in the family, Gloria allowed him to live with Frank Walker. Being a football coach, Walker saw potential in LeBron and introduced him to sports when he was only nine years old.

BASKETBALL AT ST. MARY HIGH SCHOOL

Although his journey into sports started with football, LeBron switched to basketball as he got older. When high school finally came around, James had stability as far as housing was concerned, but that was about it. In his teenage years, he faced challenges again, this time in the form of racism, as he was one of the few African American students at his school.

If you're reading this and you're in high school or junior high, you might know how devastating being bullied based on race can be. But as you will learn from LeBron, you can't let bullies hold you back. The best way to make the bullies be quiet for good is to persevere with success, and that's exactly what LeBron did.

GAINING NATIONAL RECOGNITION

In 2001, he was featured in Slam Magazine as a 6-foot-7-inch 16-year-old who could potentially be "the best high-school player in the United States." The bullies didn't have much to say at that point. But that's not all. That same year would have marked the start of his college basketball career.

It's worth mentioning here that he had offers from several institutes like the University of Miami, the University of Florida, and the University of Notre Dame. In 2003, LeBron James was the first overall pick in the NBA draft by the Cleveland Cavaliers. He was picked straight out of high school and never attended college.

LEBRON JAMES'S BASKETBALL CAREER

Despite his young age, LeBron averaged 20.9 points, 5.5 rebounds, and 5.9 assists during his first season in the NBA. He was nicknamed "The Chosen One" when he got selected for the USA team and the Today's All-USA First Team. Although he graduated from St. Mary's in 2004, he'd decided to go pro with basketball in his junior year of high school.

He became a free agent in 2010 and decided that he would play for the Miami Heat. In 2012 and 2013, he led the team to back-to-back championships and cemented his legacy as one of the all-time greats.

James went back to Cleveland in 2014 and led the team to a championship victory in 2016. He was named the NBA Finals MVP for the third time. He earned his first MVP award in the 2008 to 2009 season and his second one in the following season. He later signed with the Lakers in 2018, with the hope of raising another team to glory, but this was the time challenges came back.

Despite setbacks such as injuries while playing for the Lakers, Lebron won his fourth MVP award in the 2019-20 season and led the team to their 17th NBA championship. In February 2023, LeBron surpassed the record of Kareem Abdul-Jabbar to become the NBA's all-time leading scorer.

SINGLE-PARENT HOUSEHOLD, MEDIA SCRUTINY, PERFORMANCE PRESSURE, AND MORE

One might think that all your problems are over when you make it to the NBA. Perhaps that's what LeBron thought too. Up until his teenage years, he had battled with poverty, unstable housing, an absent father, and not being able to live with his mother. It's like life threw everything at him all at once.

LeBron has faced immense scrutiny and pressure from the media, claiming that the legend is not what he used to be. In addition, some fans who once loved him have turned against him. Needless to say, this has put some serious mental and emotional pressure on LeBron.

He has also struggled with physical injuries. While playing for the Lakers, he's experienced groin injuries, making his performance inconsistent. Despite all of this, the NBA legend has yet to hang up his sneakers. Even at the age of 38, when asked about retirement, LeBron said "no," adding "I got a lot more in the tank to give."

If there's one thing to be learned from his journey, it's the old saying "What doesn't kill you, makes you stronger!" As of 2024, LeBron has achieved over 40,000 career points. Given that "The Chosen One" has yet to retire, who knows what he'll achieve next!

LESSONS FROM LEBRON'S STORY

There are a lot of lessons to be learned from LeBron's story. Let's look at five of them.

1. The best way to make the bullies be quiet is to persevere with success.
2. Sometimes you must switch teams to find the right match.
3. You can't let the pressure of fans turning on you throw you of your game.
4. You must fight through the injuries, challenges, and adversities to reach the top.
5. If you feel like you've got more in you, then keep going.

FACTS AND QUESTIONS ABOUT LEBRON JAMES

Want to know more about LeBron James? Here are some fun facts!

1. James got married to his high-school sweetheart.
2. He's a New York Yankees fan.
3. His son is 6-foot-4-inches and is a rising star in basketball.
4. LeBron wasn't the highest-paid guy on his team until he was 31.
5. He's the cofounder of SpringHill Entertainment.

SOME TRIVIA!

It's time to test your knowledge. Can you answer these questions?

What's his mother's name?

Gloria James.

What sport did he play before basketball?

Football.

How tall was he at the age of 16?

6-foot-7-inches.

Which baseball team does he support?

New York Yankees.

When did he become a free agent?

2010.

STEPHEN CURRY
THE REVOLUTIONARY
SHOOTER

For our next story, we'll look at Stephen Curry, the basketball legend who has 400 three-pointers to his name.

One might think that being born to a father who played basketball would make for an easy life, but that wasn't the case for Steph. He has achieved magnificent triumphs in his career but fought quite a lot of battles along the way. In this chapter, we'll get to know Stephen Curry from his early childhood, talk about his problems, and see what we can learn from them.

Let's begin!

GROWING UP IN CHARLOTTE, NORTH CAROLINA.

Steph was born to Sonya and Dell Curry in 1988. His father, Dell Curry, was a successful professional basketball player. His mother Sonya, on the other hand, worked as an educator, although she had played college volleyball in her day. Given the nature of the NBA, Steph's father often moved around when he was playing for the Cleveland Cavaliers.

Steph spent his early life living in Charlotte, North Carolina. In the 1988 NBA expansion draft, Dell Curry was left unprotected by the Cavaliers and was the first pick by the Charlotte Hornets. During his father's tenure with the Hornets, he would often take young

Steph and his brother to the games. Here, they would practice shooting with the team. Steph developed his basketball IQ at a very young age. He was a star in the making, but he didn't take it for granted.

When his Dad was away scoring points, Steph's mom, who played volleyball in college, spent her time teaching him a thing or two about hoops, too. Steph was always ambitious about becoming like his father and used to practice for hours on end in the driveway.

HIGH SCHOOL DAYS AND THE STRUGGLE FOR RECOGNITION

Many of you might be in high school or junior high, and you likely know how important these years can be. The friends and memories you make will be a part of who you are for the rest of your life. But this wasn't the case for Steph. When Dell started playing for the Raptors, the family had to move to Toronto. Then, when he retired, they moved back to North Carolina.

Steph had to change schools a few times, which made things difficult with friends. But this didn't keep him from focusing on his goals. In Canada, he played basketball for Queensway Christian College, leading them to an undefeated season. And when the family moved back to the US, he attended Charlotte Christian High School, where he led the basketball team to conference titles.

Life seemed to be great for him, but he was battling demons related to living in the shadow of his father's glory. Commenting on the high expectations everyone had for him, he said, "My game and my size and my demeanor and disposition didn't match what they were looking for. My last name meant that I was supposed to be somewhere, but everything else didn't."

COLLEGE YEARS AT DAVIDSON

Can you imagine someone putting Steph Curry on the sidelines? That's hard to believe, based on what we know about him now. But that's what happened when he was in college. He had a lot of achievements to his name, but despite all this, Curry was only considered a three-star recruit. He was even called "The Baby-Faced Assassin" due to his small posture.

Steph wanted to follow in the footsteps of his father and play for Virginia Tech. However, the school was only willing to take him in as a walk-on, meaning he would have had to sit one year out. Not being able to do what his father did put a lot of pressure on Steph. But, unlike most people, he didn't give in to the pressure.

Determined to prove his worth, he attended another college that was willing to take a chance on him. While playing for Davidson, he took the underdog team to the NCAA regional final, proving the critics wrong and leaving everyone in awe.

Steph made his way to the NBA after his junior year at Davidson, as was the seventh draft by the Golden State Warriors.

ENTERING THE NBA: CHALLENGES AND TRIUMPHS

Professional sports are all about teamwork and the bond players share with each other. But this wasn't Steph's experience as he began his NBA career. His teammate, Monta Ellis, soon announced to the media that he and Steph were too small to play together. Not much team support there, right?

Steph suffered multiple injuries during his early years in the NBA. He was also criticized by people who said he didn't have the potential or skills to lead a team to glory. Self-doubt can be crippling, but it wasn't the only problem for Steph. Despite all the injuries and criticism, he refused to let others define his achievements.

Determined to fill his father's shoes, he became a four-time NBA champion as he was bestowed with the honor in 2015, 2017, 2018, and 2022. Steph also won two NBA MVP awards, one in 2015 and the other in 2016. He's also a 10-time NBA All-Star because he has played in the All-Star exhibition game since 2014 all the way to 2024.

CHANGING THE GAME

Throughout his career, Curry has faced quite a lot of challenges, both on and off the court. He suffers from a genetic eye condition that causes increased blurred vision over time. This caused him to have poor form during the 2018-19 NBA season.

He also missed the 2012 Olympics due to an injury. In addition, he suffered from ankle injuries that affected his career from 2010 to 2016, and again in April 2022.

His parents were both inspirations to him, but they got divorced in 2021, and seeing their 33-year marriage come to an end was a setback for him. Despite all this, Curry has achieved some revolutionary milestones like being a 10-time NBA All-Star and has an NBA track record that's truly unique!

LESSONS FROM STEPH'S STORY

One can learn a lot from Steph's story. Let's look at the top five lessons.

1. Failures are not the end, but rather something you can learn from.
2. What you believe about yourself is what matters.
3. The best way to silence your critics is with your performance.
4. Injuries are a part of the game, but you shouldn't let them stop you.
5. You can't let labels define you.

FACTS AND QUESTIONS ABOUT STEPHEN CURRY

Want to know more about Steph? Here are some fun facts.

1. His full name is Wardell Stephen Curry II.
2. He starred in a Burger King ad as a kid.
3. He has a verbal contract with his mother, and she fines him $100 for each turnover.
4. Curry would like Denzel Washington to play him in a movie.
5. The Baby-Faced Assassin's favorite TV show is *How to Get Away with Murder.*

SOME TRIVIA!

Think you know everything about Stephen Curry? Time for some trivia questions.

How long were his parents married?

33 years.

What sport did his mother play in college?

Volleyball.

Did Steph play in the 2012 Olympics?

No.

How much does his mother fine him for the turnover?

$100.

Steph made seventh draft for which NBA team?

Golden State Warriors.

DERRICK ROSE
OVERCOMING ADVERSITY

In our next story, we will discover the incredible journey of Derrick Rose, a basketball superstar who faced tough challenges, but never gave up. He worked hard, overcame obstacles, and always bounced back, showing us that, no matter what life throws at you, you can still reach for the stars.

In this chapter, we'll discover how Derrick turned setbacks into comebacks, dribbled through challenges, made slam-dunks of determination, and scored points through his resilience.

So, without further ado, let's get to it!

GROWING UP IN CHICAGO

Born on October 4, 1988, Derrick Rose faced tough challenges growing up in Chicago's Englewood area. Living in one of the city's most dangerous neighborhoods, he encountered daily struggles, especially financially. He lived with his mother, Brenda, and two brothers, surviving paycheck to paycheck and struggling to make ends meet.

Derrick's challenges ranged from playing on snow-covered courts to living in overcrowded homes with 10 other people, some struggling with drug issues. Despite facing adversity, his determination and resilience shone through, and he eventually became an NBA fan favorite.

HIGH SCHOOL STARDOM:
SIMEON CAREER ACADEMY

Derrick Rose's high school journey at Simeon Career Academy wasn't a smooth ride, but he worked hard to overcome losses and adhered to rules that were only holding him back. Despite his reputation as a hot prospect for college coaches, he started on the junior varsity team due to a longstanding rule that stated freshmen could not play on the varsity team.

But this didn't deter Derrick. He worked hard and the matches he played as a freshman and sophomore helped him improve his skills. Everything he had learned up until that point was tested when, during his junior year in 2006, Simeon reached the Chicago Public League championship. Despite an overtime battle in the state championship, Rose's buzzer-beater secured Simeon's first state title since 1984.

His senior year of high school basketball was filled with losses and tough games. But, despite this, Derrick's performance earned him accolades, including being named the nation's fifth-best prospect.

His remarkable high school career, marked by championship wins and personal achievements, showcased his athletic abilities and laid the foundation for the basketball superstar he would become.

COLLEGE SUCCESS AT MEMPHIS

Derrick Rose's college career at the University of Memphis had its highs on the court, but lows off it. Recruited by Coach John Calipari, Derrick chose Memphis due to its NBA player history and the mentorship provided by Rod Strickland. On the court, he led the Tigers to a remarkable season, reaching the NCAA championship game.

However, after the season, controversy affected Derrick. Allegations arose regarding an invalidated standardized test score from his high school year at Simeon. The NCAA charged Memphis with knowing Derrick had someone else take his SAT. In addition, Derrick's brother, Reggie, faced allegations of traveling with the team for free.

Despite Memphis conducting its own investigation and clearing Derrick to play, the NCAA vacated the 2007-08 season, declaring Rose ineligible. He and the university later settled with a payment of $100,000 to season ticket holders, resolving the fallout from the controversy. Derrick then decided to take a leap and enter the 2008 NBA draft after just one year of college.

NBA ROOKIE SENSATION AND MVP YEAR

Now, let's talk about Derrick Rose's journey in the NBA. Standing tall at 6 feet 3 inches and weighing in at 200 pounds, Rose was a force to be reckoned with, predominantly playing as a point guard. He showcased his prowess on the court, boasting an impressive average of 18.2 points per game.

His journey in the NBA began back in 2009. As a newcomer, he quickly made waves by clinching the NBA Rookie of the Year award, a significant achievement for any young player entering the league. He was the first player for the Chicago Bulls to score 10 points or more in 10 games since Michael Jordan.

In 2011, Rose reached a remarkable milestone when he was selected for the All-NBA team and crowned the NBA MVP of the regular season. This recognition served as a testament to his exceptional skills and dedication to the game. However, Rose's path to success was not without its challenges. He encountered numerous obstacles, including injuries and setbacks, that we'll talk about in the next section. Despite these hurdles, Rose demonstrated resilience and determination, showing us that perseverance pays off in the face of adversity.

INJURIES, SETBACKS, AND THE ROAD TO RECOVERY

Derrick Rose faced some tough injuries over the years. He was at the top of his game, but then was sidelined by a torn ACL. He had to sit out the entire next season, but he didn't let that stop him.

He worked hard to come back, only to hurt his knee again in 2013. And he suffered injuries with other teams too, including ankle and more knee injuries. But Derrick didn't lose hope. Instead of feeling sorry for himself, he focused on getting better. He became smarter on the court and changed his game.

Throughout his career, he's played for multiple teams that include the Chicago Bulls, New York Knicks, Cleveland Cavaliers, Minnesota Timberwolves, and Detroit Pistons. As of 2023, Derrick is playing for the Memphis Grizzlies. He's truly one of those NBA players with diverse experience in NBA and who knows what the future has in store for him.

We can all learn from Derrick Rose's journey. When we face tough times, we shouldn't give up. Instead, we should keep pushing forward, knowing that we can overcome obstacles with determination and hard work.

LESSONS FROM DERRICK'S STORY

Derrick's story is a source of inspiration for anyone facing challenges and setbacks. Some of these lessons include:

1. Setbacks and injuries don't define us; it's the way we bounce back that matters.
2. When challenges come, being flexible can lead to success.
3. In tough times, sometimes it helps to take it slow. Being patient, methodical, and creative can lead to remarkable achievements.
4. You can't let a negative environment impact your determination.
5. It's not just your skills that matter. Being a leader and helping others succeed makes your journey about shared victories, not just personal success.

FACTS AND QUESTIONS ABOUT DERRICK ROSE

Want to know more about Derrick? Here are some fun facts.

1. Derrick Rose was born in a tough part of Chicago.
2. Everyone in his high school called him "Mr. Basketball" because he was so good.
3. Picking a college was tough for Derrick Rose.
4. Derrick Rose made history by becoming the youngest player ever to win the MVP award.
5. Derrick Rose's favorite actor is Will Smith.

SOME TRIVIA!

If you think you know everything about Derrick Rose, it's time for some trivia questions.

Which college did Derrick Rose play for?

He played for Memphis.

What award did Derrick Rose win in his first year in the NBA?

The NBA Rookie of the Year award.

What caused Derrick Rose to miss an entire season during his career?

A torn ACL.

Which high school did Derrick Rose attend?

Simeon Career Academy.

Which NBA team drafted Derrick Rose in the 2008 NBA draft?

Chicago Bulls.

KEVIN DURANT
THE QUIET GIANT

This is the story of Kevin Durant, one of the greatest basketball players in history. Blessed with the gift of height, one might think Kevin had an easy path to becoming an NBA legend. But did you know that Kevin was bullied for his height as a child? He was quite tall in middle school which made him different from others who didn't hold back when it came to teasing him.

Kevin faced challenges in his life, but his persistence and success provide important lessons for the rest of us.

Let's dive in!

CHILDHOOD AND EARLY LOVE FOR BASKETBALL

Kevin Durant was born on September 29, 1988, in Washington, DC, to Wanda and Wayne Pratt. When Durant was just an infant, his father, Wayne, abandoned the family. Kevin was brought up by his mother and grandmother, Barbara Davis.

His brother Tony was a basketball player, and it was he who instilled a love for basketball in Kevin. Growing up, Kevin wanted to play for his favorite team, the Toronto Raptors, just like his favorite player, Vince Carter.

During middle school, when he was 10–12 years old, he was already 6 feet tall, and he was teased by his classmates for it. But he didn't let the bullies get in his head, proving that we don't have to let bullies hold us back. One of his key strengths was the love and support he received from his family.

At the age of 10, Kevin decided to become a basketball player. He joined the PG Jaguars, a team in the Amateur Athletic Union. This was where he chose the number 35 for his jersey, which is the number he uses to this day.

HIGH SCHOOL STARDOM: NATIONAL CHRISTIAN ACADEMY

During high school, he grew as much as 5 to 7 inches, causing imbalance and poor coordination. But he did not give up. He worked twice as hard and used his height as an advantage. After playing for two years for National Christian Academy, he moved to Oak Hill Academy, located in Virginia. Then, for his senior year, Kevin moved back to Maryland to support his brother, Tony, where he attended Montrose Christian School.

In his senior high school season, Kevin really showcased his talent and blew everyone away with his agility and balance, despite his impressive height. By the end of the season, he had become a national sensation and was named the Washington Post All-Met Basketball Player of the Year.

COLLEGE DOMINANCE AT TEXAS

Before deciding to go to the University of Texas, Kevin considered different options like the University of Connecticut, University of North Carolina, Duke University, University of Kentucky, and University of Louisville. However, he ultimately settled for a lesser-known program because he wanted to set his own path.

Regarded as one of the best talents to come out of high school, Kevin had a lot of pressure to succeed and live up to expectations. He could have easily crumbled under this pressure and given up on his dream, but instead he adapted to the faster and more physical style of college games and proved his worth during his freshman season.

Playing for the Texas Longhorns, he dominated on the court in the 2006 to 2007 season and was awarded with a four-seed in the NCAA tournament. During his freshman year he was also recognized as the national player of the year. He was also the first freshman to win multiple awards related to college basketball. Some of these awards include:

- Naismith College Player of the Year.
- NABC Division I Player of the Year.
- Oscar Robertson Trophy.
- Adolph Rupp Trophy.
- John R. Wooden Award.
- Big 12 Player of the Year.
- USBWA National Freshman of the Year.

Given this, we can say that hard work and unrelenting consistency prove that commitment and effort are the keys to succeeding in life.

NBA STARDOM AND THE PURSUIT OF A CHAMPIONSHIP

In 2007, Kevin realized his NBA dream when he was chosen second overall by the Seattle SuperSonics (who were renamed Oklahoma City Thunder after relocating in 2008). During his early career, Kevin won many individual awards and even Olympic gold medals, yet an NBA championship continued to elude him.

In 2016, he shifted team to the Golden State Warriors in pursuit of the elusive title, where his hunger and determination for the game only grew. Kevin's decision to sign with the Golden State Warriors was heavily criticized by the press, fans, and critics. They accused him of joining a rival team and betraying his team of nine years in search of stardom. However, Kevin saw it differently. He believed the move was a step out of his comfort zone in search of achieving the highest of honors in the NBA.

During the 2016-17 season, Kevin missed 19 games due to a Grade 2 MCL sprain and a tibial bone bruise. But his love and passion for the game were so immense that he came back at the end of the season, won the finals, and received another MVP award, teaching us that we should work hard in life and should bounce back from injuries stronger than before. The next year, he led the Golden State Warriors to back-to-back NBA titles, proving that success comes to those who work hard for it.

Controversy also followed Kevin, including a clash with his teammate in the 2018-19 season, which led to poor team chemistry. Eventually, Kevin's successful career with the Warriors ended. He decided to grow as a player and as a person, expanding his horizons with the Brooklyn Nets.

After signing with the Brooklyn Nets, he decided to take the 2019-20 season off. When he returned to the court in the following season, a hamstring injury forced him to miss 23 games. He later signed with the Phoenix Suns and is currently an active member of the roster.

LESSONS FROM KEVIN'S STORY

From failures and drawbacks to responses filled with hard work and dedication, here are the top five lessons to learn from the life of Kevin Durant:

1. Hard work and consistency are the keys to success in life.
2. Belief in your ability and trust in yourself takes you a long way.
3. You cannot let others' opinions define who you are.
4. You need to step out of your comfort zone and make bold decisions to elevate yourself to the highest level.
5. Setbacks and failures are part of life, but we can learn to overcome them.

FACTS AND QUESTIONS ABOUT KEVIN DURANT

Want to know more about Kevin Durant? Here are some interesting facts:

1. His full name is Kevin Wayne Durant.
2. He was still growing when he joined the NBA, from 6'9" to 6'11".
3. He was the youngest player to win a scoring title.
4. He is a YouTuber and video game enthusiast.
5. He was part of the team that started the production company Thirty-Five Ventures.

SOME TRIVIA!

Do you think you know everything about Kevin Durant? Here are some trivia questions:

What was Kevin's height in middle school?

6 feet.

Who was his favorite player growing up?

Vince Carter.

What college did he go to?

University of Texas.

Why did he miss 19 games during the 2016-17 season?

Grade 2 MCL sprain and a tibial bone bruise.

How old was Kevin when he chose the number 35 for his jersey?

10 years old.

I have included these free downloadable gifts to help light up your inner inspiration & reach your potential.

While you are reading through the stories, lessons and trivia, we recommend that you make use of all the bonuses we've attached here!

All our bonuses have been made specifically to help young athletes feel fired up, get inspired from the best to ever do it, and most importantly fall more in love with this incredible game!

Here's a list of what you're getting:

1) 250 Fun Facts From The World Of Sports
2) Sports Practice and Game Calendar
3) 5 Fun Exercise Drills for Kids
4) The BEST Advice From The Greatest Athletes Of All Time
5) The Mental Mindset Guided Meditation & Affirmation Collection
6) The Most Famous Events In Sports History And What They Can Teach Us

Now, it's over to you to scan the QR code, follow the instructions & get started!

CHRIS PAUL
THE POINT GOD OF THE COURT

For our next story, we'll look at the incredible life of Chris Paul, also known as "CP3" and "The Point God." He is widely regarded as one of the greatest point guards in NBA history, but gaining this reputation wasn't a walk in the park.

Initially, people thought he was too small for the NBA. Virtually the entire basketball community doubted his abilities. But Chris defied the odds and showcased remarkable energy and performance.

GROWING UP IN WINSTON-SALEM, NORTH CAROLINA

Christopher Emmanuel Paul was born on May 6, 1985, in Lewisville, North Carolina, to Charles Paul and Robin Paul. His father was a former athlete himself and imparted the fundamentals of basketball and football to Chris and his older brother C.J., encouraging their participation in team sports.

From a young age, Chris had ambitions of becoming an athlete like his father, so he and his brother dedicate hours each day to practice. In addition to his sports pursuits, Chris also worked diligently at a service station owned by his maternal grandfather, Nathaniel Jones, affectionately known as Papa Chilly. The two were very close.

Chris was a lot shorter than his peers, particularly while he was in school. However, his height did not hinder his pursuit of glory. In fact, he soon gained recognition for his speed and intelligence on the basketball court.

Unfortunately, a huge tragedy was about to take place.

HIGH SCHOOL EXCELLENCE

Chris worked hard, and his dedication earned him a spot on the basketball team at West Forsyth High School. In his junior year, he helped the school reach the state semifinals, and was named MVP of the tournament

However, tragedy struck during his senior year. The night before a crucial basketball game, Chris received devastating news—his beloved grandfather had been beaten to death by several teenagers.

It was shocking news for him, but, despite the heartbreak, he was committed to playing and helping his team win. His aunt told him to score 61 points, one for each year of his grandfather's life, as a tribute. Somehow, he managed to do it. He scored 61 points, then walked to the bench, collapsing into his parents' arms in tears.

Those 61 points in a single game and the tribute to his grandfather gained him national attention. By the end of the season, Chris was a national sensation and named North Carolina's "Mr. Basketball."

COLLEGE STARDOM:
WAKE FOREST UNIVERSITY

Chris emerged from high school widely recognized as one of the region's top talents. That was a lot of pressure and expectations for a young player. But, given what's achieved throughout his career, we can certainly say that he lived up to all the expectations.

Chris enrolled at Wake Forest University, where he joined the Demon Deacons' basketball team. During his freshman year, he not only lived up to those expectations, but surpassed them. A team leader from the outset, he broke all the school's freshman records for assists, steals, free throws, and three-point percentages.

These impressive performances earned him the title of rookie of the year in 2004. Many sports websites, including College Insider, The Sporting News, and Basketball Times, recognized him as the nation's best freshman player.

NBA CAREER: FROM THE HORNETS TO ALL-STAR STATUS

Chris eventually announced his intention to play in the NBA. He was immediately selected fourth overall by the New Orleans Hornets in the 2005 NBA Draft.

In his rookie year, his impact wasn't immediate, with the Hornets he only won 38 games. But he was still named the top Western Conference rookie every month and was ultimately crowned NBA rookie of the year.

But his true breakout year was the 2007-08 season, when Chris's on-court skills and leadership qualities secured him a spot in the NBA All-Star Game.

His consistent high-level performance and chemistry with the team propelled the Hornets to the playoffs, marking their first appearance since the 2003-04 season.

LEADERSHIP, TEAM DYNAMICS, AND THE PURSUIT OF A CHAMPIONSHIP

Fueled by his strong desire for success, Chris decided to move to the Los Angeles Clippers. This addition to the team created high hopes for the Clippers, who often played in the shadow of the Lakers.

In the following three seasons, the Clippers achieved impressive records, winning at least 56 games per year. Chris led the league in assists for two of those seasons. But despite their best efforts, the team couldn't make it past the conference semifinals in the playoffs.

By this time, Chris was in his thirties, and the signs of wear and tear started to show in his body. Chris faced a number of injuries such as a torn ligament and hamstring strains; however, he soon managed to recover.

In June 2017, Chris experienced the second major trade of his NBA career, moving from the Clippers to the Houston Rockets. His impact was soon felt by the team, as he led the Rockets to an impressive 65 wins in the 2017-18 season.

The following year, Chris suffered a hamstring injury, and the Rockets struggled early in the season. Despite having momentum entering the playoffs, the team ultimately lost to the Warriors.

In July 2019, Chris found himself on the move once again, as the Rockets traded him, along with several draft picks, to the Oklahoma City Thunder. Between 2020 and 2023, he played for the Phoenix Suns. He then spent one season at the Golden State Warriors, before moving to the San Antonio Spurs in 2024.

This NBA legend is yet to secure a championship, but his incredible track record as a 12-time All-Star speaks volumes about his achievements. Given that he's still on court, his pursuit of a championship continues. Who knows when he'll achieve that milestone or will he hang up his jersey without it?

LESSONS FROM CHRIS'S STORY

The story of Chris Paul offers numerous valuable lessons. Here are the top five:

1. Be open to new opportunities and roles, as they can fuel personal growth and make a broader impact.
2. Have faith in your abilities and trust yourself.
3. Don't let others' opinions shape your identity.
4. Strong family values and a commitment to hard work are important for achieving success in any career.
5. Injuries are bound to happen in sports, but you don't have to let them prevent you from playing and enjoying the game.

FACTS AND QUESTIONS ABOUT CHRIS PAUL

Want to know more about Chris? Here are some interesting facts:

1. He was nicknamed "CP3" by his family due to sharing initials with his father and brother.
2. He is a two-time Olympic gold medalist with the US Olympic team.
3. He is an accomplished bowler and spokesperson for the US Bowling Conference.
4. He is active with charities.
5. He has collaborated with Jordan Brand for his own line of signature shoes.

SOME TRIVIA!

Think you know all about Chris? Time for some trivia questions:

What high school did Chris Paul go to?

West Forsyth High School.

Has Chris Paul won an NBA championship?

No.

Why was he nicknamed CP3?

Because he shared initials with his father and brother.

When was Chris Paul drafted to the NBA?

In 2005.

What team did Chris Paul play for when he initially started out in the NBA?

New Orleans Hornets.

DIRK NOWITZKI
THE MAVERICK'S LEGEND

Dirk Nowitzki is a basketball superstar known for his incredible skills and loyalty to the Dallas Mavericks. Dirk played his entire 21-season NBA career with the Mavericks, earning the love, respect, and loyalty of the Dallas fans.

Despite his towering height of seven feet, Dirk Nowitzki faced his fair share of challenges. From doubts about his abilities to adapt to a new country and league, Dirk encountered obstacles that could have easily deterred him. However, he overcame these challenges and became a true icon of the sport.

In this chapter, let's lace up our sneakers and follow Dirk's footsteps as we uncover the lessons hidden within his story.

EARLY YEARS IN WÛRZBURG, GERMANY

Dirk was born into an athletic family on June 19, 1978, in Würzburg, Germany, with a mother who excelled in basketball and a father who was a handball player. In addition, Dirk stood out among his peers due to his towering height, which suggested he had a future in sports. However, he faced criticism and hurtful comments from others, even being called a "freak."

Thankfully, Dirk embraced his passion for sports, initially trying his hand at tennis and handball. When he caught the attention of Holger Geschwindner, a former professional basketball player, Dirk's sports journey truly began. Under Holger's guidance, Dirk started rigorous training, focusing on developing his shooting and passing skills.

Joining the DJK sports club's squad at just 16, Dirk encountered challenges in the competitive Second Bundesliga league. Despite his talent, he was benched and struggled with academic pressure, diverting his focus from the game. However, he was determined to overcome these obstacles and pursue his dream of becoming a basketball star.

His journey took a significant turn when he participated in the Nike "Hoop Heroes Tour," where he showcased his skills against NBA stars like Charles Barkley and Scottie Pippen, earning praise and recognition on an international stage. Dirk didn't just play— he outplayed Barkley, and even dunked on him! Barkley was impressed and said, "The boy is a genius. If he wants to enter the NBA, he can call me."

TRANSITION TO THE NBA: CHALLENGES AND TRIUMPHS

Transitioning to the NBA wasn't all smooth sailing for Dirk Nowitzki. He was the ninth draft pick by The Milwaukee Bucks in 1998 and was then traded to the Dallas Mavericks.

The 1998-99 season brought its share of challenges, starting with a delayed start due to a lockout. That's when the league's owners collectively decided to shut down operations and suspend league activities.

In addition, at just 20 years old, Dirk questioned his readiness for the big leagues. But despite his doubts, he made his NBA debut. He initially faced criticism after missing his first shots and failing to grab rebounds.

Despite a tough start, he played 47 games, showcasing his potential with an average of 8.2 points per game. While adjusting to the NBA, Dirk found solace in his friendship with Steve Nash, who was a source of support and camaraderie through the ups and downs. They trained together, faced challenges, and grew better every year.

Despite the setbacks, Dirk persevered. His determination to learn from mistakes and grow stronger each game was evident as his remarkable performance throughout his entire NBA career.

NBA MVP, FINALS MVP, AND CHAMPIONSHIP GLORY

Dirk Nowitzki's journey to NBA glory wasn't without its hurdles. Despite his remarkable achievements, he faced challenges that tested his resilience and determination. A foot injury suffered in a preparation game for EuroBasket 2003 posed significant setbacks, impacting his performance and raising doubts about his ability to lead the Mavericks.

Fortunately, Dirk navigated the highs and lows of professional basketball, emerging stronger and more focused. Each setback became an opportunity for growth, teaching him invaluable lessons about perseverance and mental toughness. He remained steadfast in his pursuit of excellence, refusing to let obstacles derail his dreams.

Dirk was the first European to be named the NBA's MVP, joining the ranks of legends like Hakeem Olajuwon and Steve Nash. He was also one of only 19 players to bag both the regular season and NBA Finals MVP awards in 2011 as he played for the Mavericks! This was the year when Dirk led the Dallas Mavericks to their first-ever NBA championship.

As Dirk's success in the NBA increased, he witnessed a change in the game. Throughout his entire NBA career, he won countless awards like the NBA Finals MVP in 2011 and the NBA MVP in 2007 and is a 14-time NBA Star.

LEADERSHIP, LOYALTY, AND LEGACY

Dirk Nowitzki's connection with Dallas wasn't always smooth sailing. He faced tough times, but stood tall, leading his team through both victories and defeats. Displaying loyalty, he stayed with the Mavericks for his entire career, guiding them to 11 consecutive NBA playoffs. He even sacrificed higher salaries!

Outside the NBA, Dirk inspired his nation, leading Germany to Olympic glory and winning a bronze medal. In 2011, Dirk was named the German Sports Personality of the Year, a first for a basketball player. And in 2012, he became the first non-American player to be awarded the Naismith Legacy Award.

Dirk's story teaches us about perseverance, loyalty, and the power of chasing your dreams, showing that with determination, anything is possible.

LESSONS FROM DIRK'S STORY

Here are some valuable lessons we can learn from Dirk's incredible journey from Germany all the way to the NBA.

1. Never let labels define what you can do.
2. Hard work and dedication can turn doubts into slam dunks.
3. Loyalty is a powerful force that builds lasting connections.
4. Playing for the team can lead to victories that go beyond personal records.
5. Being able to adapt to changing circumstances is necessary.

FACTS AND QUESTIONS ABOUT DIRK NOWITZKI

Want to know more about Dirk? Here are some fun facts.

1. Dirk Nowitzki ranks seventh in NBA history for win shares. That's the number of times a player's performance contributes to the team's wins and Dirk has surpassed basketball legends like Kobe Bryant, Shaquille O'Neal, Oscar Robertson, and LeBron James.
2. You won't believe this, but Dirk Nowitzki isn't much of a beer fan.
3. Throughout his NBA career, Dirk Nowitzki has only managed two triple-doubles, showcasing his focus on specific skills rather than all-around stats.
4. Dirk gave up a whopping $194 million in potential salaries to keep his team strong. He didn't pursue maximum contacts or higher salaries That's a big sacrifice for the love of the game and his team.
5. Between 2012 and his retirement in 2019, Dirk Nowitzki didn't dunk in a playoff game.

SOME TRIVIA!

If you think you know everything about Dirk Nowitzki, it's time for some trivia questions.

How tall is Dirk?

7 feet tall

What did Dirk Nowitzki earn when he led the German Olympic basketball team in 2002?

A bronze medal.

How many seasons did Dirk Nowitzki play (a rare feat in the NBA)?

21 seasons.

In which month was Dirk Nowitzki born?

He was born in June.

What position was Dirk Nowitzki drafted in the 1998 NBA draft?

He was drafted at the ninth.

KAWHI LEONARD
THE SILENT FORCE

In this chapter, we will look at the life of Kawhi Leonard, one of the best NBA defenders of all time. Kawhi came from a sporting family, and people might assume that he had it easy in his pursuit of the NBA dream, but he actually missed the basketball tryouts when he was in high school because he wasn't aware of the actual time and location! And that was just one of the many challenges he overcame on his way to greatness. In this chapter, we'll walk a mile in his shoes and see what we can learn from him.

Let's check out his story!

GROWING UP IN RIVERSIDE, CALIFORNIA

Kawhi Leonard was born on June 29, 1991, to Mark Leonard and Kim Robertson in Los Angeles, California. He was the only boy in the family but had four older sisters. When Kawhi was just five years old, his parents split up. It can be difficult for kids when their parents separate. Fortunately, Kawhi had sports to keep him focused.

The love for sports ran in the Leonard family. Kawhi's father was a high school football player and the cousin of Stevie Johnson who is one of the most famous NFL players ever. Growing up, Kawhi fell in love with both football and basketball—football due to his father who was an athlete in high school.

Life as a teenager was not always easy for Kawhi. During his junior year, Kawhi lost his father in a tragic assassination. He was shot and killed in Compton. The killer was never found and the motive behind the murder remains unknown. Distraught and devastated at the loss of his father, Kawhi still played the next night against Dominguez Hills at the Pauley Pavilion.

The talent that Kawhi possessed was on display in his senior year when he was named California's Mr. Basketball. Despite his potential for basketball, he didn't receive many college scholarships.

COLLEGE SUCCESS AT SAN DIEGO STATE

During his freshman year at San Diego State, Kawhi had to leave home at 5 am for workouts so he would not have to miss classes. His commitment, dedication, and passion for basketball was what kept him going.

The unrelenting hard work and determination paid off for Kawhi. During his first year playing college basketball, his team won the Mountain West Conference. In his sophomore year, he led his team to an almost flawless season, once again winning the Mountain West Conference tournament.

Kawhi shows us that talent alone is not enough until we work hard enough to realize that potential. Waking up at 5 am in the morning for workouts so he wouldn't miss his classes is just one example.

NBA STARDOM: DEFENSIVE PROWESS AND CHAMPIONSHIP GLORY

Kawhi's NBA career began with a few setbacks and challenges. He was initially drafted by the Indiana Pacers as the 15th pick; however, on December 10, 2011, after the NBA lockout, he signed a multimillion-dollar deal with the San Antonio Spurs.

Kawhi was not initially a starter and had to wait to be promoted among those playing on the court. It's worth mentioning that this promotion only came because of Richard Jefferson being traded to the Golden State Warriors for Stephen Jackson. After the trade, Kawhi was promoted to the starting small forward positions, and Stephen Jackson was his backup.

When Kawhi finally got his chance to play for the Spurs, he showed the world what an unbelievable talent he was. During his first year, he was named to the NBA All-Rookie First Team!

Kawhi's ambitions were not just to make it to the NBA, but to win championships. During his third year, he made that dream a reality. In the 2013-14 season, Kawhi led his team to an NBA championship, where he was named MVP. This was one of the greatest accomplishments in NBA history.

The following season, Kawhi added excellent defensive abilities to his already illustrious gameplay. He faced some ups and downs during this season as he suffered from blurry vision due to an infection in his right eye caused by conjunctivitis. In addition, he had also injured his right hand, causing him to miss 15 games.

Upon his return, he helped the Spurs secure wins over the Portland Trail Blazers and the Golden State Warriors. As a result of these performances, he was the NBA Defensive Player of the Year. It's worth mentioning that Kawhi is the only player, alongside Michael Jordan and Hakeem Olajuwon, to win both NBA Defensive Player of the Year and NBA Finals MVP.

He remained with the San Antonio Spurs for seven seasons, winning multiple awards, including 2013-14 finals MVP, and two-time All-Star selection.

INJURY SETBACKS, TEAM CHANGES, AND MEDIA SCRUTINY

Injuries are an inevitable part of every athlete's career, and Kawhi was no exception. During the 2017-18 season, he missed the first 27 games due to a right quadriceps injury. His teammates and the Spurs management had disputes over his rehab program. Kawhi Leonard had missed a significant amount of the 2014-15 season due to injury, so he wanted to be extra cautious on his rehab and injuries. His slow rehab made the fans question his loyalty to the team.

The media added to the criticism, saying that Kawhi had let his team down by not showing up for games, even when he was fit to play. Due to this controversy, Kawhi ended up moving to the Toronto Raptors in 2018.

Kawhi ultimately overcame his critics by winning a second NBA championship in his first year with the Raptors. As this incredible comeback demonstrates, you shouldn't let critics put limits on what you can achieve!

LESSONS FROM KAWHI'S STORY

1. Setbacks and failures in life are opportunities to improve ourselves.
2. Hard work and consistency are the keys to a successful life.
3. We must put in 100% of our effort if we want to achieve big goals.
4. Leadership isn't always about being vocal, sometimes it's about leading with examples of performance.
5. We must never give up on our dreams, no matter how many setbacks or failures we face in life.

FACTS AND QUESTIONS ABOUT KAWHI LEONARD

Want to know more about Kawhi Leonard? Here are some interesting facts:

1. His full name is Kawhi Anthony Leonard.
2. He holds the record for the most points scored in a game by a San Antonio Spur.
3. Leonard's uncle, Dennis Robertson, is his chief business strategist.
4. Leonard's father owned a car wash in Compton, California.
5. He won two NBA championships in his career.

SOME TRIVIA!

Think you know everything about Kawhi Leonard? Try these questions!

What is Kawhi Leonard's nickname?

The Klaw.

What car did he own during his college years?

A silver Chevy Malibu.

Who are some famous celebrity friends of Kawhi Leonard?

Lil Wayne, Kendrick Lamar, and YG.

Where was Kawhi father assassinated and was the killer ever found?

He was assassinated in Compton and the killer was not found.

How old was Kawhi when he lost his father?

16.

GIANNIS ANTETOKOUNMPO
THE GREEK FREAK

Giannis Antetokounmpo is an NBA champion and one of the most dominant basketball players of the modern era. Throughout most of his childhood, he had to battle financial struggles because his parents didn't hold work permits. At a young age, he had to sell items on the street with his brother to make ends meet. He eventually found a savior in basketball because sports pretty much ran in the family.

In this chapter, we will explore the inspiring life journey of Giannis Antetokounmpo and see what lessons we can learn from him.

Let's get started!

EARLY LIFE IN ATHENS, GREECE

Giannis Antetokounmpo was born on December 6, 1994, in Athens, Greece, to two immigrant parents who had emigrated from Lagos, Nigeria, three years earlier. Growing up, Giannis had a life that was very different from most basketball players.

His parents did not hold work permits in Greece, so they could not find work very easily. For this reason, he and his older brother had to sell items on the streets of his neighborhood, Sepolia, to help out his parents. Fortunately for Giannis, he had sports in his blood. His father was a soccer player in Nigeria, while his mother was a high jumper. Whenever things felt overwhelming, Giannis could turn to his love of sports for stress relief. He developed a special love for basketball and began playing in 2007, when he was 13.

As a child, Giannis felt like an outsider in both the Greek and Nigerian cultures. While his household was predominantly Nigerian, his outside life was dominated by Greek culture. He was stuck between two worlds, trying to fit in while going through the normal challenges of adolescence.

Up until the age of 18, Giannis couldn't travel outside the country and had no papers from Greece or Nigeria. However, on May 9, 2013, he was issued Greek citizenship. It's worth mentioning that this was two months before the NBA draft. His entire early life is a life lesson for us to never give up on the difficulties and problems that life throws at us. If we work hard enough for a goal, only then can we achieve it.

NBA RISE: FROM DRAFT DAY TO MVP

After playing a couple of years in the Greek second division, Giannis decided to make himself available for the NBA draft in 2013. The time had come for Giannis to realize his lifelong dream of becoming a player in the world's biggest basketball league. His hard work paid off, because he was drafted by the Milwaukee Bucks, signing a rookie scale contract.

Giannis was only 18 when he made his NBA debut. In fact, he was one of the youngest players to play an NBA game, at 18 years and 311 days. He signed his rookie contract with the Milwaukee Bucks on July 30, 2013. During his Rookie season, he averaged 6.8 points, 4.4 rebounds, and 1.9 assists in 77 appearances. When the season ended, he was named to the 2013-14 NBA All-Rookie second team.

He spent the next six years practicing and playing hard, and between 2018 and 2020, he was the NBA MVP for two consecutive seasons.

BECOMING A CHAMPION: THE MILWAUKEE BUCKS JOURNEY

As much as winning MVP made Giannis a fan favorite, he was never one for individual awards. His only career goal was to become an NBA champion. He was all about the team effort, and has played his entire career for the Bucks.

After his second MVP-winning season in 2019-20, he wanted to go one better and win the NBA championship for his team. He re-signed with the Bucks and led his team to a third-place finish. However, Giannis suffered an injury during the playoffs when he twisted his right ankle. Prior to that, he actually got suspended for one game without pay for headbutting Moritz Wagner of the Washington Wizards.

He fought through the pain and returned for the finals, only to put in one of the best performances of his life, winning the Bucks their first NBA championship in 50 years. All of the hard work he had put in paid off as he made his dream of being NBA champion come true.

LANGUAGE BARRIERS, ADAPTING TO THE NBA, AND LEADERSHIP

Coming from a non-English-speaking background, Giannis struggled with a language barrier that instilled a fear of speaking out during his early years. He told the press, "Early in my career, I was really quiet, and with the language barrier, it was harder for me. I felt like I'd say the wrong thing, I'd say something stupid, so I just chose not to talk at all."

In addition, he had grown up playing in Greece, where the style of play is far different from the hard-hitting and challenging style in the NBA. Being only 18 when he was drafted into the NBA, Giannis had to adapt his gameplay and his personality to succeed, teaching us an important lesson that challenges in life can be overcome when we face them and adapt ourselves to the changes.

He overcame the language barrier and was eventually named captain of the Bucks. The life and career of Giannis prove that success does not depend on where we come from, but rather how hard we work and how much effort we are willing to put in.

LESSONS FROM GIANNIS'S STORY

1. Sometimes, language barriers can make things difficult, but we can't let them hold us back.
2. Never give up on your dreams, even if they seem impossible. Always keep striving for improvement.
3. Facing challenges head-on and adapting to new environments allows us to grow and succeed.
4. Success comes from effort and determination.
5. We must believe in our ability and stay loyal to those who are there for us at our worst times like Giannis did with the Bucks

FACTS AND QUESTIONS ABOUT GIANNIS ANTETOKOUNMPO

Want to know more about Giannis? Here are some fun facts:

1. His full name is Giannis Sina Ugo Antetokounmpo.
2. He holds two different nationalities: Greek and Nigerian.
3. He is the only non-American player to win NBA MVP twice.
4. Giannis served in the Hellenic Army in Greece.
5. Giannis has only played for the Bucks throughout his NBA career.

SOME TRIVIA!

Think you know everything about Giannis? Try this trivia quiz!

How old was Giannis when he was drafted in to the NBA?

He was 18 years old.

Why did Giannis and his brother have to sell items on the street?

Because their parents were immigrants and didn't have work permits.

On what date did he sign his rookie contract?

July 30, 2013.

At what age was he given Greek citizenship?

At the age of 18.

Why was Giannis quiet early in his career?

He had a language barrier and was afraid he'd say the wrong things.

I have included these free downloadable gifts to help light up your inner inspiration & reach your potential.

While you are reading through the stories, lessons and trivia, we recommend that you make use of all the bonuses we've attached here!

All our bonuses have been made specifically to help young athletes feel fired up, get inspired from the best to ever do it, and most importantly fall more in love with this incredible game!

Here's a list of what you're getting:

1) 250 Fun Facts From The World Of Sports
2) Sports Practice and Game Calendar
3) 5 Fun Exercise Drills for Kids
4) The BEST Advice From The Greatest Athletes Of All Time
5) The Mental Mindset Guided Meditation & Affirmation Collection
6) The Most Famous Events In Sports History And What They Can Teach Us

Now, it's over to you to scan the QR code, follow the instructions & get started!

RUSSELL WESTBROOK
THE TRIPLE-DOUBLE MACHINE

In this chapter, we'll discover the story of Russell Westbrook, a point guard who played for five different NBA teams. Russell's journey since early childhood has been filled with countless ups and downs. One of them was the death of his friend Khelcey. Both dreamed of playing for UCLA together.

Throughout this chapter, we'll look at everything he faced while growing up in Los Angeles. We'll also dive into his college life and NBA career, learning lessons from his experiences and success.

Let's get to it!

GROWING UP IN LOS ANGELES

Russell Westbrook was born on November 18, 1988, in Long Beach, California. He fell in love with playing ball when he was young. Along with his childhood friend, Khelcey Barrs, Russell dreamt of going to UCLA to play basketball. Sadly, while life had greatness in store for Russell, his friend's fate was a bit different.

In 2004, Khelcey passed away due to an enlarged heart. At the time, Russell was only 16 years old. Facing such a tragedy at such a young age can be demoralizing for a person, oftentimes causing them to suffer from depression. Russell was devastated by his friend's death, but it did not stop him from working toward his dreams.

During high school, he was 5-feet-8-inches tall and only weighed around 140 pounds. His size was a bit of a disadvantage on the basketball court, and he didn't make the varsity team until his junior year at Leuzinger High School. Russell didn't reach his full adult height of 6-feet-3-inches until his senior year, but by then he'd already put in a lot of hard work and made a name for himself.

He wanted to play for UCLA, in memory of his best friend, but opportunities didn't immediately present themselves. He didn't receive much attention from recruiters, but eventually caught the eye of Ben Howland, a basketball coach at UCLA, and was offered a scholarship.

COLLEGE SUCCESS AT UCLA

Receiving a scholarship made it possible for Russell to play at UCLA, but he didn't receive a hero's welcome when he first started there. He wore the number 0 and was only selected as a backup for Darren Collison.

He stayed in that position throughout his entire freshman year. However, Russell wasn't going to let this break his spirit. He was determined to move up and become a starter and worked incredibly hard in the weight room and the gym.

A year later, Collison was injured, and it was time for Russell to show the world what he was capable of. After phenomenal performances, he was named All-Pac-10 Third Team and won the Pac-10 Defensive Player of the Year.

Russell knew he had what it took to make it big in professional basketball. After spending two years at UCLA, Russell decided not to finish college, but instead to enter the NBA draft in 2008.

NBA CAREER: THUNDER DAYS
AND MVP SEASON

Russell made his NBA debut in 2008. Since then, he has played for five NBA teams: the Oklahoma City Thunder, Houston Rockets, Washington Wizards, Los Angeles Lakers, and Los Angeles Clippers.

Russell stuck with the Thunder for 11 seasons and became a unique and versatile player for the team. His run with the Thunder helped shape his NBA career but did not come without challenges. A few years after his debut, he suffered a knee injury during a collision with another player. He later found out that he needed surgery and was declared unfit for the season.

While Russell was determined to prove his worth, he had to undergo two additional surgeries, which kept him from returning for quite some time. After such a long wait, he was hoping for a dream comeback, but he only played for a few minutes and had to sit out every other game. But the next year, he put in a phenomenal performance and was named MVP.

Over the next few years, he ended up switching teams' numerous times. On July 16, 2019, he was traded to the Houston Rockets for Chris Paul and a few other players. But the move for him served as a reunion with former teammate James Harden. His debut game with the Rockets resulted in a loss and a few months later, in 2020, he tested positive for COVID-19.

However, Russell recovered and returned later that same month, only suffering from another injury: a strained right quad. Toward the end of 2020, he was traded to the Washington Wizards in place of John Wall. While playing for the Wizards, he became the first player since Magic Johnson to record a 30–10–20 triple-double with 35 points.

In 2021, Russell was traded to the Los Angeles Lakers for Kentavious Caldwell-Pope, Kyle Kuzma, Montrezl Harrell, and the draft rights to Isaiah Jackson. It's worth mentioning that this was the third time he was traded in three years. He's been with the Lakers since 2021, so who knows, maybe another switch is around the corner!

CRITICS, TEAM CHANGES, AND PERSONAL ACHIEVEMENTS

Throughout his NBA career, Russell won numerous awards, including the NBA MVP and being named an All-Star. But he was also heavily criticized for being selfish and not playing for his team. In addition, during his run with the LA Lakers, the team didn't perform as expected.

Russell and his family were heavily criticized, and his wife even received death threats. This criticism affected his kids and his marriage, but Russell has never let critics, injuries, or personal setbacks keep him from reaching his goals. He promised himself that he would achieve greatness in memory of his childhood friend, Khelcey, and he has done exactly that.

LESSONS FROM RUSSELL'S STORY

There's a lot that can be learned from Russell's story:

1. Tragedies are a part of life, but they can be overcome.
2. You can't let the critics get to you and hold you back.
3. Your family and kids always come first no matter what.
4. You must be willing to fail if you want to achieve greatness.
5. Hard work pays off, no matter what you are facing in life.

FACTS AND QUESTIONS ABOUT RUSSELL WESTBROOK

Are you eager to know more about Russell? Here are some fun facts!

1. He started his own fashion line called Honor the Gift.
2. Breakfast is his favorite meal of the day.
3. Number 4 is his favorite number, and he wore it in high school too.
4. His motto since high school has been "Why Not?"
5. Russell didn't miss a single game in his first three seasons with the NBA.

SOME TRIVIA!

Think you're a Russell expert? Try these trivia questions!

What was his best friend's name?

Khelcey Barrs.

What sport did his wife play?

She also played Basketball.

How many NBA teams has he played for?

Russell has played for 5 NBA teams.

How old was he when Khelcey died?

16 years old.

How tall was Russell when he started high school?

He was around 5-feet-3-inches tall.

KOBE BRYANT
A BASKETBALL LEGEND'S
ENDURING IMPACT

Let's look at one of the most famous basketball players of all time, Kobe Bryant. Not many people have achieved as much as Kobe did during his life, but his journey from Philadelphia to the NBA was filled with countless ups and downs. He grew up in Italy and didn't know the language, then moved to the US and became fluent in English.

Apart from this, he also faced some severe criticism from the media for his performance and things he had to deal with off the court. However, Kobe managed to overcome these challenges, turn his dreams into reality, and serve as a role model for others. There's a lot that can be learned from his story, so let's get started.

GROWING UP IN PHILADELPHIA

Kobe Bryant was born on August 23, 1978, in Philadelphia. He was the youngest of three siblings and was the only son of former NBA player Joe Bryant. His uncle, John "Chubby" Cox, was also an NBA player. Kobe grew up in Italy and he spent quite a lot of time alone and suffered from racism. However, he did manage to make a few friends while playing basketball and soccer.

Kobe moved back to the United States in 1991, unaware that a new set of challenges awaited him. While in the US, Kobe struggled with English, since he had spent so much time abroad where he had faced language barriers too. If it hadn't been for basketball, Kobe would not have fit in and his life would have been very different. But Kobe was obsessed with hoops and put in tons of effort every day. He improved his game, and eventually became one of the best players in history.

HIGH SCHOOL STARDOM: LOWER MERION HIGH SCHOOL

Kobe attended Lower Merion High School, joined the basketball team, and quickly began to make a name for himself. But Kobe wasn't just good with the ball. He excelled in academics and had an SAT score of 1080, meaning he could easily get into almost any college he wanted. But Kobe had something entirely different in mind. He wanted to go pro straight out of high school.

This decision received a lot of publicity, and not all of it positive. But Kobe didn't let other people's opinions change his plans. He ignored the critics and did what he said he was going to do.

NBA DOMINANCE: CHAMPIONSHIPS, SCORING TITLES, AND OTHER ACHIEVEMENTS

In 1996, at the age of 17, Kobe was drafted by the Los Angeles Lakers. At the time, he wasn't legally an adult, so his parents had to co-sign the contract with him. Later, at the age of 18, he signed a rookie contract with the Lakers worth $3.5 million. It's worth mentioning here that Kobe, before being drafted by the Lakers, had practiced quite a lot and had honed his craft.

He'd play against former Laker players Larry Drew and Michael Cooper in Los Angeles during practice in 1996. According to Jerry West, who was the general manager of the Lakers at the time Kobe "marched over these people." From 1996 to 2016, the year in which he retired, Kobe only played for the Lakers.

Over the years, he carried the team to numerous championships. He also won MVP awards and an Olympic gold medal; with many people saying he was the best basketball player since Michael Jordan. During the start of his debut season, Kobe only played for a limited number of minutes, but gained more playing time as the season continued.

However, during the playoffs of the seasons, Kobe ended up shooting four air balls, which led to loss for the Lakers. Despite this, Shaquille O'Neal, who was playing for the opposing team, commented that Kobe was the only player with the guts to take shots like that. Throughout 1999 to 2002, he became a premier shooting guard in the league.

It was during these years when he earned appearances in the league's All-NBA, All-Star, and All-Defensive teams. During 2002 to 2004, Kobe's performance wasn't at par, and he was facing some problems in his personal life off the court, which made him the target of media scrutiny and criticism.

During 2004 to 2008, Kobe saw quite a few ups and downs, like the Lakers not being in playoff for the first time in 10 years, their coach leaving and then coming back, and being able to play in an NBA All-Star game.

INJURIES, CONTROVERSIES, AND PERSONAL GROWTH

In 2008, Kobe led the Lakers to the NBA finals for the first time without Shaq playing on the team. But the Lakers ended up losing the series. This resulted in a lot of criticism of Kobe, as his ability to be a team player and secure a championship without Shaq by his side was called into question.

During 2013 to 2015, Kobe faced several injuries that included an Achilles tendon rupture, knee fracture, and torn rotator cuff. As a result of the injuries, Kobe had missed several games. However, despite beginning on the sidelines, fans still voted to see him in his 16th All-Star game. During his final season, he suffered a calf injury, which led to him missing two games.

On April 13, 2016, he played his final game, scored 60 points, and become the only player to do so in a single game. Kobe continued to work hard and serve as a role model for the rest of us. After living the life of a legend, Kobe passed away in a tragic helicopter crash, along with his daughter and a few other family friends. They were travelling to Camarillo Airport in Ventura County for a basketball game at Mamba Sports Academy in Thousand Oaks. However, due to severe weather conditions, the helicopter crashed into the side of a mountain in Calabasas. Kobe left behind countless memories and lessons all of us can learn from.

LESSONS FROM KOBE'S STORY

There are a lot of valuable lessons one can learn from Kobe's story:

1. Hard work and dedication always pay off.
2. You can't let the critics get inside your head.
3. Your work ethic is what matters.
4. When faced with setbacks, you must be willing to work things out.
5. Pressure and challenges are an opportunity to rise higher.

FACTS AND QUESTIONS ABOUT KOBE BRYANT

Want to know more about Kobe? Here are some fun facts!

1. He was named after a Japanese steak.
2. He scored 81 points in a single game.
3. Kobe was the youngest player ever to win the NBA Slam Dunk Contest.
4. He never lost a game while playing for Team USA.
5. He made a surprise appearance at a Taylor Swift concert.

SOME TRIVIA!

Do you think you know all about Kobe? Try these trivia questions!

How old was Kobe when he passed away?

41.

How much was his rookie contract for?

$3.5 million.

What sport did he play other than basketball?

Soccer.

When did he move back to the US?

1991.

When was he drafted in the NBA?

1996.

DWYANE WADE
THE FLASH'S IMPACT

For our next story, we'll look at the extraordinary life of Dwyane Wade, aka "The Flash." He is widely praised as being one of the greatest shooting guards in NBA history. But achieving this stardom was no easy feat. From a young age, Dwyane faced challenging circumstances that no child should have to endure, yet he remained steadfast in pursuing his goals.

In this chapter, we'll explore Dwyane's incredible career and discuss the challenges and hardships he had to overcome to become the person we know today. We'll talk about his childhood and see what lessons we can learn from his life.

Let's dive into the remarkable story of Dwyane Wade.

GROWING UP IN CHICAGO

Dwyane Tyrone Wade Jr. was born on January 17, 1982, in Chicago, Illinois, to JoLinda and Dwyane Wade Sr. When he was just four months old, his parents separated, and JoLinda gained custody of him and his 5-year-old sister, Tragil. The family faced financial struggles, eventually relying on welfare for support.

Things got worse when JoLinda developed an addiction to alcohol, cigarettes, cocaine, and heroin. Dwyane often witnessed his mother using or dealing drugs at home. However, his life took a huge turn for the better when his sister convinced him to live with his father and stepmom.

Basketball was Dwyane's sport from childhood, and this new setting helped him nurture that passion. He eventually ended up attending Harold L. Richards High School, where his older stepbrother, Demetrius, had already made a mark as the star of the basketball team.

Dwyane looked up to his brother and sister, but he also looked up to basketball legend Michael Jordan. He modeled his playing style after Jordan and earned a spot on the varsity team during his junior year, eventually emerging as the team's new star.

COLLEGE SUCCESS AT MARQUETTE

When it was time for college, Dwyane chose to go to Marquette University in Milwaukee, Wisconsin. However, his academic scores were quite low, so he was ineligible to play during the first season. Head Coach Crean nevertheless accepted him as a partial qualifier. This meant that Dwayne could attend school and practice with the team.

Dwyane hit the books, improved his grades, and came roaring back during his sophomore year. In the 2001-02 season, he owned the court, leading his team, the Golden Eagles, to a 26-7 record in Conference USA. Then, in 2002-03, Wade turned up the heat even more, scoring an average of 21.5 points and steering his team to an impressive 27-6 record.

The highlight of his college career was a triple-double against Kentucky that shot Marquette into the Final Four for the first time since 1977. In case you didn't know, a triple-double is when you score double-digit points in three different categories like points, rebounds, and assists. During the game, Dwyane scored 29 points, 11 rebounds, and 11 assists.

It's worth mentioning that this was the fourth triple-double ever to be recorded in NCAA history. As a gesture of respect,

Marquette broke the rules to retire Wade's jersey in 2007 before his graduation.

MIAMI HEAT GLORY DAYS

The success and fame that Dwyane garnered in college led him to skip his senior year and enter the 2003 NBA draft, where the Miami Heat immediately selected him as the fifth overall pick. His rookie year with the Heat was incredible. He averaged 16.2 points, 4.5 assists, and 4.0 rebounds. This led to his unanimous selection for the 2004 NBA All-Rookie team. He also placed third in Rookie of the Year voting, behind LeBron James and Carmelo Anthony.

His statistics only went up when Shaquille O'Neal joined the Heat, averaging 24.1 points and 6.8 assists per game. Then, in 2006, he achieved his dream by winning the NBA championship after delivering an exceptional performance in the finals against the Dallas Mavericks. His outstanding display earned him the NBA finals MVP honor.

Dwyane went on to secure three NBA titles with the Miami Heat. His unwavering dedication to the game and fueled his desire to improve and perform at his best. This is a powerful lesson, that success isn't handed out, but is the result of continuous hard work and dedication.

INJURIES, TRANSITIONS, AND OFF-COURT CONTRIBUTIONS

Dwyane suffered some serious knee issues throughout his career, but he didn't let that stop him. Not only did he win three NBA championships, but he also emerged as a serious contender for the title of the league's second-best shooting guard, giving Kobe Bryant a run for his money.

In 2007, Dwyane suffered severe shoulder and knee injuries requiring multiple operations. Injuries like this can be career-enders for many players, but he wasn't about to let them stop him from doing what he loved. He worked harder than ever before, and the following year, he came back stronger than before. He averaged 30.2 points per game and secured his first NBA scoring title.

"The Flash" eventually transitioned from being a player to a team owner with stakes in two teams: the Utah Jazz and Chicago Sky. He was given that nickname by Shaquille O'Neal when the two teamed up in Miami due to his speed and agility on the court.

His impact is felt on the court and off-court. He has shown extensive support for social justice and provided resources for communities in need. He also stands by his unwavering stance against gun violence and his advocacy for LGBTQ+ rights. Along with this, he also has ownership stakes in Utah Jazz and WNBA's Chicago Sky.

Whether playing basketball, contributing to society, or taking on some business ventures like ownership stakes in basketball teams, Dwyane Wade proves that it's possible to make an impact.

LESSONS FROM WADE'S STORY

Dwyane Wade's story offers many valuable lessons. Here are the top five:

1. You shouldn't be afraid to advocate what you believe in.
2. Sometimes a change in your environment can help you nurture your passion.
3. Use your platform for positive change in the community.
4. You can turn your childhood passion into a professional career just like Dwyane.
5. Make an impact beyond your field by committing to excellence in all aspects of life.

FACTS AND QUESTIONS ABOUT DWYANE WADE

Want to know more about Wade? Let's reflect upon some facts.

1. Dwyane is a devoted Christian and wears number 3 in tribute to the Holy Trinity.
2. He donates 10% of his salary to charity.
3. After his NBA career, Dwyane launched a men's fashion line.
4. He participated in the Olympics twice.
5. Dwyane is married to actress Gabrielle Union.

SOME TRIVIA!

Do you think you know everything about Dwyane Wade? Here are some trivia questions:

In what city was Dwyane Wade born?

He was born in Chicago, Illinois.

How many NBA championships did Dwyane Wade win with the Miami Heat?

He won 3 championships.

Which university did Dwyane Wade attend before entering the NBA draft?

He attended Marquette University.

What post-retirement ventures has Dwyane Wade been involved in?

Ownership in NBA teams, fashion entrepreneurship, and philanthropic initiatives.

Beyond basketball, what other areas does Dwyane actively advocate for?

Social justice and educational initiatives.

CARMELO ANTHONY
FROM BROOKLYN TO THE NBA

In this chapter, we'll look at the life of Carmelo Anthony. Highly celebrated as one of the most prolific scorers in basketball history, he has been a true model of consistency. But was it smooth sailing for him? Just like many other players we've discussed in previous chapters, he had his own struggles on the way to glory.

In this chapter, we'll explore his life and career, discussing the hurdles he overcame and learning lessons from his journey.

Let's get started.

GROWING UP IN BROOKLYN

Carmelo Kyam Anthony was born on May 29, 1984, in Brooklyn, New York, to Carmelo Iriarte and Mary Anthony. He was just an infant when his father passed away. His mother took care of him and his three older siblings, working as a housekeeper to provide for the family.

The family eventually moved to Baltimore, which was a rough city with a lot of drugs. But Mary kept a strict household, prioritizing education for her children. Carmelo was motivated to excel in school. He also began playing basketball.

Carmelo attended Towson Catholic High School but was frustrated when he didn't make the high school basketball team his first year. Instead of giving up, he decided to focus and work hard to get better.

By his sophomore season, he had grown a lot. He was taller and had developed his skills to the point that he was well-known in the local area. During the summer of 1999, he had grown nearly half a foot tall and was 6 foot 5 inches. He had turned things around with hard work and determination. In his junior year, he doubled his numbers and scored 26 points and 10.3 rebounds.

COLLEGE STARDOM AT SYRACUSE

Noticing his potential, college coaches from across the country began to take interest. By his junior year in high school, Carmelo had committed to playing for Syracuse University. He had to switch high schools to meet academic requirements and transferred to Oak Hill Academy. The transition was tough, as it took him out of his comfort zone. He had to leave behind friends and venture into a new environment. But Carmelo embraced the challenge and did his best.

Carmelo improved his test scores and basketball skills, becoming the highest-ranked high school basketball player in the country. He enrolled at Syracuse in the fall of 2002 and quickly adapted to college basketball standards.

As the top player for the Syracuse Orange, he led the team to their first national championship in the spring of 2003, with a win over the University of Kansas. He was named the tournament's most outstanding player, then declared his intention for the upcoming 2003 NBA draft.

SCORING TITLES AND TEAM TRANSITIONS

Carmelo entered the NBA as the third overall pick in a talent-filled draft, alongside stars like LeBron James and Dwyane Wade. He was excited to get picked by the Denver Nuggets, but also acknowledged the pressure that came with playing in the NBA.

Nonetheless, he was open to the challenge that made an immediate impact during his rookie season.

After a remarkable stint with the Nuggets, he moved to the New York Knicks in 2011, returning to his hometown. During his run with the Nuggets, he scored 40 points in a game becoming the second youngest player in NBA history to do so. He was only 19 years old at the time. Carmelo played a key role in the team achieving an impressive 54-28 record during the 2012-13 season.

However, his relationship with the team eventually soured, leading to his departure. Carmelo enjoyed stints with different teams, facing unique challenges along the way, but his commitment to the game and his performance never wavered. He stuck with the New York Knicks until 2017 and in the 2012 to 2013 season he averaged 41.8 point in four games. It's worth mentioning here that no other player had scored up to 35 points in five straight games since Kobe Bryant in the 2006-07 season.

PLAYOFF STRUGGLES, TEAM DYNAMICS, AND PERSEVERANCE

Carmelo switched teams but failed to win a championship. Some questioned his ability to lead a team to crucial victories and success in the playoffs. Some blamed his playing style, as he often preferred to score by himself rather than passing the ball to his teammates.

This criticism led to Carmelo changing teams frequently, seeking new opportunities to find success. In 2017, he was traded to the Oklahoma City Thunder, followed by a brief stint with the Atlanta Hawks before being released. Carmelo then joined the Houston Rockets, playing only 10 games before being traded to the Chicago Bulls.

Released by the Bulls in January 2019, he remained unsigned until the Portland Trail Blazers signed him to a one-year contract in November 2019. Switching teams this often was challenging for him. He alluded to this when he said, "It's challenging to kind of stay strong and positive through all this." But he showed resilience and never stopped working hard.

In 2023, Carmelo decided to retire after an amazing 19-season career in the NBA. He holds the distinction of being the ninth-leading scorer in NBA history. In a post-retirement interview, he said that he had no regrets whatsoever about not winning the championship.

He emphasized that he had given his all and said he felt at peace with his career. His attitude reminds us that we shouldn't let the one thing we didn't achieve overshadow all our other accomplishments.

LESSONS FROM CARMELO'S STORY

Here are the top five lessons to learn from the life of Carmelo Anthony:

1. Continuous learning and adaptability are key to a successful career.
2. It is important to maintain a good attitude through both wins and losses.
3. You can't let the frustration of rejection hold you back. You must be willing to work hard.
4. Dedication and hard work will pave your way to success.
5. You cannot let others' opinions define who you are.

FACTS AND QUESTIONS ABOUT CARMELO ANTHONY

Want to know more about Carmelo Anthony? Here are some interesting facts:

1. He has been chosen for the NBA All-Star Game 10 times.
2. He actively supports education and communities through his foundation, The Carmelo Anthony Foundation.
3. During the 2012 Summer Olympics, he set a record for the most points in a single game by an American player.
4. He is a leading scorer for the Knicks.
5. He is a three-time Olympic gold medalist, winning the 2008, 2012, and 2016 Games with the US basketball team.

SOME TRIVIA!

Let's test what you know about Carmelo Anthony. Here are some trivia questions.

How many teams has Carmelo Anthony played for in the NBA?

Throughout his career he played for 6 teams.

Has Carmelo Anthony won any NBA championships?

No, he hasn't won any NBA championships.

What work of philanthropy has he been involved in?

He is involved in improving educational opportunities for underprivileged youth.

How tall was Carmelo Anthony during the summer of 1999?

He was 6 foot 5 inches tall in 1999.

Did he win any gold medals?

Yes, he won 3 Olympics gold medals.

JOEL EMBIID
DOMINATING THE PAINT

The story of Joel Embiid is one that's filled with lots of ups and downs. One of the main challenges he faced growing up was the toxic environment in Cameroon. But his dedication to academics and sports is what kept him safe from it.

Born in Cameroon, he initially wanted to become a volleyball player when he was young. However, he ended up becoming an NBA legend. Joel has achieved some remarkable milestones throughout his career, but also overcome lots of challenges. In this chapter, we'll dive into his story, look at all the challenges he's faced, and see what can be learned from him.

Let's begin!

EARLY LIFE IN CAMEROON

Joel Embiid was born in Yaoundé, Cameroon, to Thomas and Christine Embiid. His first foray into sports was with volleyball and soccer. Believe it or not, the NBA star initially wanted to play professional volleyball in Europe.

Growing up in Cameroon was challenging for him. The country struggles with corruption, poverty, and violence, and wasn't an ideal platform for someone working toward a professional sports career.

Joel was a great student who worked hard. As a child, his schedule included 10-hour schooldays and homework until midnight. He was also actively involved in sports. He started playing basketball at the age of 15 and modeled his game after NBA Hall of Famer Hakeem Olajuwon.

He was eventually discovered at a basketball camp by Luc Mbah-a Moute, an NBA player who began to mentor him. A year later, Joel moved to the United States, where he devoted himself to basketball.

COLLEGE DAYS AT KANSAS

You might think that his problems of growing up in a toxic environment would have ended when he came over to the US. However, when he came to the US, the 16-year-old was pretty much on his own. He couldn't speak English and didn't know anyone. Before making a name for himself in basketball, he was mocked by others around him, to the point where he was demoralized.

He spent time alone, crying and thinking about giving up, but rededicated himself to working hard and silencing everyone who mocked him. Before attending college in Kansas, he'd led his high school basketball team to the state championship.

In college, he had initially given up on basketball because he was outplayed. It got to a point where he went to the coach and asked to be sidelined. However, he soon found the strength to believe in himself again. He attributed a huge part of his college basketball career success to his ability of self-belief and the power of the mind.

Finding his strengths once again, he started to excel. In his college basketball career, he played 28 games and scored over 15 points in 7 of them. Given his performances, he was named one of the 30 finalists for Naismith College Player of the Year. However, soon after, he suffered a stress fracture in his back and missed out on the NCAA tournament.

NBA STARDOM: OVERCOMING INJURIES AND DOMINATING THE PAINT

Joel declared his intention for the NBA draft, but was ruled out for six months, because he had to undergo back surgery. Later, he was taken as the third pick for the Philadelphia 76ers, making him one of only three NBA players from Cameroon.

After signing his first contract, he had to miss out on his first two NBA seasons due to a foot injury and delayed recovery. Experiencing such a setback at the start of a career might make some people want to give up, but Joel wasn't like other players. He had the strength, courage, and self-belief to persevere.

He eventually debuted as center for the 76ers. Due to his great performance, he was named to the World Team for the 2017 Rising Star Challenge and the Eastern Conference Rookie of the Month. The following season, he was a starter for the NBA All-Star game.

During 2018-19, he battled flu-like symptoms and illnesses, causing him to miss a few games. Although he made it into the playoffs, his performance wasn't up to scratch, which led to disappointment for the Sixers in the playoffs. The next year, he was suspended for two games due to an on-court conflict. Despite all these setbacks, he managed to focus on his game, and became the NBA MVP runner-up in 2021. The next year, he put in his career-best performance, winning the title of NBA MVP.

INJURIES, CRITICISM, AND LEADERSHIP RESPONSIBILITIES

Joel Embiid is one of those players who's had quite a rough journey. He grew up in a country that was filled with corruption and violence and later moved to one where he was a stranger. In

Cameroon, Joel was dedicated to his academics and sports and didn't have many friends.

After moving to the US, he was relieved, given that school was easier. However, Joel wasn't familiar with American culture and didn't know much English, which kept him from having a social life. His NBA career was filled with injuries and setbacks, but he managed to persevere through it all. He had an injury-plagued season in 2016 to 2017. During the time, one of the most severe injuries he faced was a torn meniscus in his left knee. Due to this injury, he had to undergo surgery.

In the following season, he faced an orbital fracture of his left eye and had to undergo surgery, which kept him off the court for two weeks. In the 2018-19 season, he had to miss 14 games total due to a sore knee. He became an MVP runner up in the 2020-21 season. However, in the following season, he again faced an orbital fracture and a thumb injury, which required surgery.

But all of this couldn't hold him back, as he ultimately gave historic performances and was named the NBA MVP.

LESSONS FROM JOEL'S STORY

As he once said, Joel Embiid's story was "literally like a movie." Here are five lessons we can learn from his story:

1. You can't let circumstances beyond your control dictate your life.
2. It's common to be mocked by others, but you can't let that hold you back.
3. You need to make decisions based on what you value.
4. Things may not work out the way you want, but you can't give up.
5. Sometimes, you have to take a leap of faith, like Joel did when moving to the US.

FACTS AND QUESTIONS ABOUT JOEL EMBIID

Want to know more about Joel? Here are five fun facts you might not know:

1. Joel is a skilled rapper.
2. He has his own clothing line called "Uncle Drew."
3. Joel has been featured on the cover of *Vogue* magazine.
4. He was named one of *Time* magazine's "100 Most Influential People."
5. He has a foundation that provides support to underprivileged youth in Cameroon.

SOME TRIVIA!

Do you think you know all about Joel? Try these trivia questions!

What sports did he play before basketball?

Volleyball and soccer.

What's his clothing line called?

Uncle Drew.

In which season did he win the NBA MVP?

The 2022-23 season.

Where did he go to college?

Kansas State University.

Who does he consider to be his basketball role model?

Hakeem Olajuwon.

DAMIAN LILLARD
THE TRAILBLAZER'S
CLUTCH PERFORMER

Not many in the NBA have had a career like Damian Lillard's. In this chapter, let's explore his incredible career. We'll start our journey in Oakland, learning about his childhood before moving on to his years on the court, learning lessons along the way that we can apply in our own lives.

Let's get started!

GROWING UP IN OAKLAND

Damian was born in 1990 to Houston and Gina Lillard. He spent his early life in Oakland, where things could get rough at times. The neighborhood he lived in was a common place for drugs and crime. But this didn't keep him from achieving his goals. Damian was keen on pursuing basketball as a career from a very young age.

He has stated that it was his family's love, care, and compassion that kept him from getting into trouble. He went through several high schools, hoping to find one with a basketball program where he could excel. He eventually ended up transferring to Oakland High. During this time there, he performed remarkably on the court, averaging a little under 20 points per game.

COLLEGE SUCCESS AT WEBER STATE

When it was time for college, getting into a reputable school was a challenge for him. He didn't receive many scholarships offers because recruiters believed he lacked potential. But Damian didn't let these rejections get the better of him. He began to play for his local teams, as he believed that it would help him get better and allow him to gain the attention of college recruiters.

Damian still didn't get any college offers from major Division I schools, but all the hard work eventually paid off when he received an offer from Weber State University. He wasn't about to let this opportunity go to waste.

Damian started performing from day one, keen to prove his skills, leadership abilities, and work ethic. He led his college basketball team to numerous victories and quickly became one of the top players in the country.

During his freshman year, he averaged 11.5 points per game and was even named Big Sky Conference Freshman of the Year. He continued to work hard and a year later averaged 19.7 points per game as he led the Wildcat to the conference championship. However, at the time, he suffered a foot injury that caused him to miss 10 games.

But he came back stronger than before and averaged 24.5 points in his junior year. Despite such an impressive improvement, he still came in second to Reggie Hamilton Oakland University. Some might have lost hope after working hard and coming in second place, but Damian Lillard wasn't one of those people.

The best performance of his college career came on December 3, 2011, when he scored 41 points in a single game against San Jose State. At this point, he was gaining widespread recognition for his performances. Damian skipped his senior season at Weber State and entered the NBA draft of 2012. Although Damian had decided to skip his senior season at Weber State, he did complete his sales degree from the university in 2015.

CLUTCH MOMENTS AND ALL-STAR STATUS

Despite his performances, Damian was always thought of as an underdog. Fortunately, he didn't let that label get to him. All the hard work and effort he put in helped him make a name for himself, and he soon caught the attention of NBA scouts.

Damian was the sixth overall pick for the Portland Trail Blazers in the 2012 NBA draft. Once with the team, he excelled during his first season in the NBA. His performance earned him a spot in the All-Star festivities during which he became the first player in NBA history to take part in five events. These events include the Rising Stars Challenge, Skills Challenge, Three-Point Contest, Slam Dunk Contest, and the All-Star Game.

Throughout his career, Damian received several prestigious awards, including the Magic Johnson Award, NBA Teammate of the Year, seven All-Star selections, and the NBA Rising Star award.

After playing for seven seasons straight, Damian had to sit out for around 30 games in 2019-20 due to groin injuries he faced in December and January. He had managed to avoid any major problems at the time by choosing to take a rest, but tragedy was right around the corner.

In 2021, Lillard suffered a significant abdominal problem and he had to undergo major surgery. It was a severe setback to his career and he missed the entire season. This also had an impact on Portland, because the team didn't make it to the playoffs for the first time since they'd drafted Damian.

True to form, however, Damian didn't let the challenge get to him. Instead, he came back stronger than ever before and gave one of the best performances of his career by scoring a season high of 39 points, along with 7 assists and 3 blocks.

PLAYOFF BATTLES, TEAM DYNAMICS, AND ELEVATING TEAMMATES

Given that he's led the Portland Trail Blazers to the playoffs six times, Lillard truly has a reputation like no other, which makes his abilities unquestionable. As far as his overall performance in the playoffs is concerned, he's played in 61 games.

During the four play-off games in 2020, he managed to score 24.3 points, 4.3 assists, and 3.5 rebounds. But that is not all. You see, Damian is also loyal to his team. He even came out and said "See this the type I am. I would never fold under anything. I'll sink with the ship, I'll go down. That's how I would do it."

But, despite all of his injuries, he managed to bounce back stronger than ever before and led the roster to glory once again.

LESSONS FROM DAMIAN'S STORY

There are a lot of lessons to be learned from Damian's career. The top five include:

1. Keep exploring until you find the right option.
2. You can't let what others say about you get in your head.
3. Don't let circumstances define what you can achieve.
4. Failure and rejection aren't the end of the road.
5. You can use setbacks to come back stronger.

FACTS AND QUESTIONS ABOUT DAMIAN LILLARD

Want to know more about Lillard? Check out these fun facts!

1. Damian is afraid of historic statues.
2. He lived with his mother during his NBA years.
3. He created the RESPECT program to help local kids graduate high school.
4. Damian was a two-star prospect coming out of high school.
5. He's the highest-paid player in Trail Blazer history.

SOME TRIVIA!

Do you feel like you know everything about Lillard? Try these trivia questions.

Which high school did Damian Lillard attend?

Oakland High.

What was his points average in high school?

20 points.

How many times has he been an NBA All-Star?

Seven times.

How many games did he miss due to an injury?

He missed 30 games in 2019 and 2020 combined.

Has he won an MVP?

No, he has not won any MVP awards.

KYLE LOWRY FROM THE HARDWOOD TO LEADERSHIP TRIUMPHS

In our final chapter, we will learn about Kyle Lowry, an NBA champion and an All-Star six years in a row. During his NBA career, Kyle has achieved what most can only hope for; however, Kyle had to work for his success and he has never backed away from a challenge. Get ready to learn from one of the greats!

GROWING UP IN PHILADELPHIA

Kyle was born to Marie Holloway and Lonnie Lowry Sr. on March 25, 1986. Born and raised in north Philadelphia, he had a rough time as a child. His father lived just 10 minutes away from him and his elder brother but was not a part of their lives. Meanwhile, his mother had to work two jobs to make ends meet.

Without either of his parents around much, Kyle would likely have gone down a troubled path if it weren't for his older brother, Lonnie Jr., who stepped in and served as a sort of father figure. Lonnie Jr. kept Kyle from getting into trouble. He's also the one who taught Kyle to play basketball.

Both found solace in the sport, which filled the void left by their father's absence. Lonnie Jr. would search through newspapers looking for basketball tryout ads and would ensure that Kyle made it to the tryouts.

Kyle developed a talent for basketball at a young age, and soon caught the attention of Dave Distal, an assistant high school coach. Dave convinced Kyle to attend Cardinal Dougherty High School, where he excelled and made a name for himself. He received the Pennsylvania High School Player of the Year award and was ranked the sixth best high school point guard in the entire United States.

COLLEGE DAYS AT VILLANOVA

Kyle decided to attend Villanova University, where he played on the basketball team and continued to improve. However, he had some issues with authority figures, including his coaches. It got to the point where one of the coaches had to tell him that if any of the teammates said he was causing problems.

The message eventually got through to Kyle, and he stopped getting in his own way. He played for the Villanova Wildcats during his freshman and sophomore years and gave phenomenal performances on the court. He soon began receiving national recognition and was named to the First Team All-Big 5 and the All-Big East Second Team.

NBA CAREER: LEADERSHIP, CHAMPIONSHIPS, AND ALL-STAR APPEARANCES

Despite his abilities and accomplishments in college, Kyle wasn't a top choice in the NBA, although he still managed to land the 24th overall pick in 2006's NBA draft. That year, he made his debut with the Memphis Grizzlies. But after playing just 10 games, he ended up breaking his wrist in a match against the Cleveland Cavaliers.

After undergoing surgery, he came back and performed better than before. However, further disappointment was waiting for him in the next season, when the guard position he was competing for was given to Mike Conley Jr. by their new coach.

Kyle was later traded to the Houston Rockets. Then, the following year, he became a restricted free agent. The Cleveland Cavaliers made an offer of $23 million to sign him, but the Rockets matched it.

During his NBA career, he has also played for the Raptors, the Miami Heat, and the Hornets, and has earned multiple awards, including NBA champion, All-NBA Third Team, NBA All-Star, and an Olympic gold medal. In 2016, his performances helped the Raptors get to game 6 of the Eastern Conference Finals, but he was unable to get them to game 7. However, during that game, he scored 35 points. His performance earned him his first spot on the All-Star NBA team.

It's worth mentioning that Kyle is one of the only players in franchise history, alongside Vince Carter and Chris Bosh, to have achieved this milestone. His first NBA championship came during the 2018-19 season. During game 6 of the season, he scored 26 points, 10 assists, and 7 rebounds, leading the Raptors to their first championship win in history.

Along with these achievements, Kyle has also been an NBA All-Star for 5 years in a row from 2015 to 2020. He's also played for the US men's national team and won a gold medal in the summer 2016 Olympics.

TEAM CHANGES, PERSEVERANCE, AND THE PURSUIT OF EXCELLENCE

Kyle has had a memorable run in the NBA up until now, but one that's been filled with countless ups and downs. Throughout his entire career, he's been no stranger to injuries and battled quite a lot of knees, elbow, and back problems and has gone through quite a lot of team changes.

His journey into the NBA started with Grizzlies back in 2006 and he played with them until 2009. At that time, he was traded to the Houston Rockets in a three-team deal between the Grizzlies and the Orlando Magic. Kyle played with the Rockets until 2012, but in his final year he ended up missing 16 games.

This was the time when he was hospitalized due to a bacterial infection. Toward mid-2012, he was traded to the Toronto Raptors in exchange for Gary Forbes. He played with the Raptors for nearly a decade during which he achieved remarkable milestones like being an NBA All Star for five years and a championship.

In 2021, he was traded to the Miami Heat in exchange for former teammate Goran Dragić and Precious Achiuwa. While playing for the Heat, he recorded his first triple-double by scoring 20 points, 12 rebounds, and 10 assists against Utah Jazz. However, the following year, he had to miss multiple games due to a hamstring injury.

In 2024, Kyle signed with the Philadelphia 76ers. Who knows what he'll achieve next!

LESSONS FROM KYLE'S STORY

Kyle's career has been full of highlights, but he had to work hard to navigate challenges and injuries. Here are some of the lessons we can learn from him:

1. Make the most of what life gives you.
2. Learn to be patient; you can't have it your way all the time.
3. Life happens, but you need to be able to remain focused on your goals.
4. Injuries, setbacks, and challenges are part of the game.
5. You can't let the circumstances you're born into define who you become.

FACTS AND QUESTIONS ABOUT KYLE LOWRY

Do you want to know more about Kyle? Here are some fun facts.

1. He scored 56 points in his rookie season.
2. He was traded to Toronto for Gary Forbes.
3. Kyle has his own beverage line called "FamJuice."
4. Kyle has had his own signature shoe with PEAK.
5. In addition to basketball, he loves playing golf.

SOME TRIVIA!

Think you know everything about Kyle? Here are some trivia questions!

Has he ever won an Olympic gold?

Yes, in 2016.

Kyle was an NBA All-Star for how many years in a row?

Six.

What sport did his wife play in high school?

Basketball.

What was the name of his college coach?

Jay Wright.

Who taught him to play basketball?

His brother.

CONCLUSION

In this book, we have gotten to know 15 inspiring stories about modern basketball legends like LeBron James, Steph Curry, Kobe Bryant, Damian Lillard, and more. These players, and others we have covered, have one thing in common—they have all faced challenges and managed to overcome them.

While they all had their own specific circumstances and problems, they proved that it isn't the challenges that matter, but what you choose to do about them. That's one of the most important things in life. If you let challenges take control, you'll be stuck in the same place. So, if you're facing a tough time right now, know that you have what it takes within you!

Remember Giannis? He had a challenging childhood because his parents didn't have work permits and he along with his brother had to sell items on the street. But he didn't give up. He did what it took and that's exactly what mattered. You might not be able to stop challenges from coming into your life, but you can get rid of them.

Remember when we talked about LeBron James being bullied because of his race? He chose not to let the bullying get in his head, and instead silenced everyone with his performance on the court.

Bullying is something that many of us will face in life. We need to take inspiration from LeBron and learn how to keep our cool. What would have happened had LeBron not been able to maintain his composure? What if he had lashed out and had an argument or a fistfight? He may have been suspended from high school and compromised his entire basketball career.

The lesson to be learned here is that you can't let others provoke you. Keep your head down, block out the bullies, keep grinding, and sooner or later your success alone will be enough to silence them.

Another valuable lesson we learned in this book is that you can't let circumstances define what you become. Many of the players we covered were born into unfavorable circumstances. Some were born in regions filled with violence, poverty, corruption, and drugs. Others experienced the loss of a loved one at a very young age or had family problems.

Task Russell Westbrook, for example, who lost his friend at a very young. Both dreamed of becoming basketball greats when they were young. The death of a friend had to have taken a toll on Russell, but he didn't let that hold him back. He not only made it to college basketball, but became an NBA legend.

You might be going through something similar. If you are, know that whatever it is you're facing is not your fault. However, having said that, it is your responsibility to decide how to deal with your circumstances.

If you don't want your situation to define what you achieve and become, you must take action. You must practice for hours on end, like Kobe Bryant, to bounce back, like Steph Curry, and to persevere, like Damian Lillard. It's all about what you choose to do.

All the players you learned about were just like you at one point in their lives. What helped them succeed was focus, dedication, and hard work. These three things are the building blocks of success. Without them, no one has ever achieved true success in life.

All these basketball players are legends. They are some of the best to ever play the game. But if you look closely, you'll see that the reason for their success is that they have worked harder than other people.

Whether in basketball or other areas in life, if you want to be like them, that's exactly what you need to do. Putting in the hard work each day can be challenging, and there may be external circumstances holding you back. But regardless of your situation, remember all the life lessons you've learned throughout this book, including:

- Believing in yourself is what matters most.
- Seeing challenges as opportunities is what counts.
- Having an unshakable work ethic will take you far in life.
- Working hard and being dedicated to a goal will pay off.
- Seeing failures as lessons, not end results, is what matters.
- Success is the best way to silence the critics.
- Letting what others say get to you doesn't do you any good.
- Having the ability to deal with challenges and adversity will get you to the top.
- Looking for opportunities helps you find success.
- Taking responsibility for your actions is key.

Remember all these lessons and know that dreams are only as big as the people who pursue them. One of the biggest obstacles to success is fear of failure, but if you want something bad enough, you'll be willing to work hard and risk making mistakes to get there. Believe it or not, fear is something that'll make the most talented and capable people question themselves.

But what you need to know is that it's not the fear that matters; it's what you do with the fear that does. Think about it for a second, do you think any of these players would have made it big if they were afraid. Most of them faced severe injuries but didn't let fear take over and quit. They persevered, they bounced back, they became better than before, and achieved greatness.

To become a legend, you must believe in yourself and what you want to achieve in life. When you're able to do that, you'll begin to see opportunities. You'll find courage and strength. You will act, fail, learn, and go at it again. You will succeed!

Now that we've reached the end, remember to learn from these stories, focus on your goal, and, before you know it, your dreams will become reality.

Good luck!

Printed in Great Britain
by Amazon